Reading J…

A Beginner's Guide

Julie Woods

Lecturer in Old Testament and Biblical Hebrew

GROVE BOOKS LIMITED

RIDLEY HALL RD CAMBRIDGE CB3 9HU

Contents

1 Introduction 3

2 Beginning with Jeremiah 5

3 Jeremiah's Words 9

4 Jeremiah's Life 14

5 God Engaged 17

6 The Others 19

7 The End, the Conclusion and Beyond 23

Notes 26

Dedication

Dedicated to Mo Sharratt and Mel Welch, friends of faith and fun, with whom I started the 'theological' journey (with RB). Thank you for all your support, encouragement and affirmation in different ways since then.

Note

Unless otherwise indicated, biblical quotations are from the ESV.

First Impression December 2020

ISSN 1365-490X

ISBN 978 1 78827 146 2

1 Introduction

Poor Jeremiah! In forty years of preaching, he was subject to hatred, abuse, mockery and persecution. He was thrown into a cistern, beaten, put in stocks, had his writings burned up by the king and people wanted to kill him. In order that his life be an object lesson of his message, God required him not to marry and there was a period when he was not permitted to go to weddings and funerals. If the people had repented then maybe it would have been an easier burden, but they did not. Had God actually carried out the punishment that Jeremiah was threatening, decade after decade, then maybe the prophet would not have been so mocked by his family, friends and enemies for his message. Nor, perhaps, would he have felt deceived by God as he did at least once. Jeremiah had a hard life in most respects. That is not to say that Jeremiah was without support or that his life was one of joyless bleakness, however.

We do not know what Jeremiah thought at the end of his life, but he could have been forgiven for thinking that he had put everything into serving God, but that it was all for nothing, because the people eventually went into exile due to their wickedness. What he could not have foreseen is that his words would be preserved for thousands of years and that while his reputation, even now, is that of the 'weeping prophet,' many believers would be able to quote some of his words: '"For I know the plans I have for you," declares the LORD, "plans to prosper you and not to harm you, plans to give you hope and a future."' (Jer 29.11 NIV). Would he, who had his words burned by a king, be surprised to know that today, his words are used as encouragement to others? Two and a half thousand years later, Jeremiah is one of the most moving figures in the Bible.

Jeremiah is one of the most moving figures in the Bible

The Book of Jeremiah is the longest in the Bible in terms of word count, although it does not have the most chapters, so it is impossible to cover everything here. Instead, this book will look at some of the more well-known passages or ones that are characteristic and representative of Jeremiah, overall. I will group the material according to subject matter, rather than work through Jeremiah in chronological or canonical order, particularly since the chronological/canonical order does not seem to be especially significant in the case of Jeremiah.

In the next chapter, I will look at Jeremiah's call, and then will take his words as the subject of the third chapter, covering the so-called Temple Sermon (Jer 7.1–15), the critique of kings and prophets (Jeremiah 21–23, 27–28), Jehoiakim's burning of the scroll (Jeremiah 36) and the 'Book of Consolation' (Jeremiah 30–31). The fourth chapter will concentrate on Jeremiah's life, namely his lament in chapter 20 and some of his symbolic actions. Chapter Five will then focus on God's engagement with humans as shown in his weeping over them, and his responsiveness to them as explained in Jeremiah's visit to the potter's house (Jeremiah 18). I will deal with foreigners in the following chapter, particularly Ebed-Melech (Jeremiah 38), and the oracles against Babylon (Jeremiah 50–51) and Moab (Jeremiah 48). The concluding chapter will cover the final chapter of Jeremiah (Jeremiah 52).

I will address issues of genre, form and tone, along with other theological interests and issues that have been of major significance in the field of OT studies, as and when they arise. Sometimes, I will give short readings of passages by way of example of how one might interpret Jeremiah. There are a number of themes that run throughout Jeremiah that help to give the book a different character from the other prophetic books and these will be noted where they occur in the passages under examination. Some of these themes are: deception and falsehood (the Hebrew word is *sheqer*); plucking up, breaking down, destroying, overthrowing, building and planting; turning / repenting; and the 'foe from the north.' At this point, it is pertinent to turn to the text of Jeremiah itself.

Jeremiah has a different character from the other prophets

Beginning with Jeremiah

2

Superscription (Jer 1.1-3)

The Book of Jeremiah is so named because it contains the words of Jeremiah, as specified in the opening verses—the superscription (Jer 1.1–3). Many prophetic books have such a superscription, which gives the name of the prophet (in this case Jeremiah, son of Hilkiah) and usually other details, such as where the prophet came from (Jeremiah was from Anathoth, just north of Jerusalem), at what time in history he was speaking (Jeremiah had a long ministry from the days of King Josiah, King Jehoiakim and King Zedekiah until the exile of Jerusalem) and to whom he was speaking (sometimes made apparent by reference to the kings—these kings mentioned in Jer 1.2–3 were kings of Judah and are explicitly specified as such in the superscription). The superscription in Jeremiah is a long one and other prophetic books may have few of these details. Some books, like Jeremiah, contain superscription-like phrases later in the book, such as 25.1; 27.1; 32.1; 36.1 and 49.34.

The superscription most likely acted as an authoritative stamp on the work—the people could trust it because the words within were attributed to established prophets whom God had entrusted with his words. Nowadays, whether they explicitly recognize it, people tend to trust the Bible/God's word/Scripture because it is canon. The canon was established in part because ancient believers recognized the enduring value of some books and preserved as Scripture those books in which they most clearly heard the word of the LORD.

It is worth noting as a point of clarity that the superscription does not mean that every word in the Book of Jeremiah was spoken or written by Jeremiah and the book tells us that itself. Jeremiah 51.64 ends with, 'Thus far are the words of Jeremiah'—then comes Jeremiah 52. Like most biblical books, the Book of Jeremiah consists of material gathered together, edited and added to. Scholars have often deemed the Book of Jeremiah to have been edited by the deuteronomistic editors, those writers responsible for the deuteronomistic history (that is, the books of Joshua, Judges, Samuel and Kings).[1] By whatever means the text of Jeremiah came together, however, that which Jews and Christians work with now in their faith-based communities is the final, or received, form of the text.

When and Where

We have already noted that Jeremiah preached through the reigns of the Judean kings Josiah, Jehoiakim and Zedekiah until the time of the Babylonian exile. The year when Jerusalem, the most important city of Judah, fell to Babylon was in 587 or 586 BCE. Jeremiah prophesied for roughly the last forty years of Judah's history as a nation and monarchy, and his ministry was primarily to this southern kingdom of Judah. Just to clarify, the twelve tribes of Israel split after Solomon's reign into two kingdoms—the northern kingdom of Israel (ten tribes) and the southern kingdom of Judah (two tribes). By the time of Jeremiah, the northern kingdom of Israel had already gone into exile—about a hundred years before the start of Jeremiah's ministry—and now the southern kingdom was facing a similar situation. Whereas Assyria had taken Israel into captivity, the southern kingdom of Judah was facing the threat of Babylon. When Judah did fall to Babylon, Jeremiah was eventually carried to Egypt by his own people where, we presume, he ended his days, for he was elderly by then (Jer 43.6).

Poetry and Prose

In terms of style of writing, the Bible can be split very broadly into two: poetry and prose. The majority of biblical prophetic utterances are written in poetry. Most English Bibles make it easy to see at a glance which parts the translators consider to be poetry and which are prose because poetry is indented and each poetic phrase is begun on a new line, leaving considerable white space around the edges, while prose goes to the edges of the column of text. A ruler can run down the edges of prose and each line will just touch the ruler. That is not the case for poetry. It is not always easy to distinguish between Hebrew poetry and prose, so there might be slight differences across translated versions.[2] The Hebrew poetry of the Old Testament is a whole subject in itself, but a few pointers can stand a beginner in good stead.[3] Hebrew poetry does not rhyme or follow a meter, though there can be meter to Hebrew poetry. Instead it often follows a system of parallelism where two lines (sometimes more) echo each other, frequently in similarity to each other, though sometimes in contrast. Usually, each line has two parts to it and each of those parts is echoed in the next line. Take Jer 1.5 as an example:

Before I formed you in the womb	I knew you
And before you were born	I consecrated you

Through the repeated idea in parallelism, the ideas are emphasized. Here, the emphasis is on the, perhaps surprising, idea that God did not consecrate Jeremiah only after he saw what an aspiring young prophet he was, but before he was even born—while he was in his mother's womb. Not only was he known by God, but consecrated, that is, he was set aside for sacred ministry by God. By such repetition, the poetry also slows the reader down and makes them dwell a little longer on what is being said. One of Ellen Davis's recommendations is to read the biblical text more slowly, for 'Reading the text more slowly is essential for learning to love the Bible.'[4]

The book of Jeremiah contains more prose than any other prophetic book, in terms of narrative, and we learn more biographical details about Jeremiah than any other prophet. Unfortunately, this has led some in the past to attempt to create a psychological or character profile for Jeremiah. There is too little information about him for this to be viable. What we are given are snapshots over a long period of time. Nevertheless, we are able to see how Jeremiah responded as a human to various events in his life. As fellow humans beings, we can easily resonate with some of Jeremiah's responses, though far removed from him in terms of history and (probably) geography.

Jeremiah's Call and Message (Jer 1.4–10)

Like other biblical characters, for example, Moses, Gideon, Samuel, Isaiah and Ezekiel, Jeremiah receives a specific call to his ministry. When God calls Moses, he is present in the burning bush, but when God reveals himself to Jeremiah it is not spectacular. Jer 1.4 simply reads, 'Now the word of the LORD came to me, saying.' The reason that God calls a person is because he has a task for them, and God tells Jeremiah, 'I appointed you a prophet to the nations' (Jer 1.5b). Like Moses and others who are called by God in the Old Testament, Jeremiah feels that he is inadequate and expresses his objection; 'Ah, Lord GOD! Behold, I do not know how to speak, for I am only a youth' (Jer 1.6). God assures Jeremiah that he will be the one giving him the words and that Jeremiah is not to fear.

These stories of being called—'call narratives,' as they are termed—demonstrate that God's servant has, indeed, been divinely commissioned to do his work. It is in the call narrative that we learn that Jeremiah has been consecrated since before birth. Call narratives often follow a pattern—as already noted, in most call narratives the servant objects to God's commission.[5] One function of patterns such as these is that where a story departs from them, it may indicate some significance.

It is not unusual for call narratives to contain words and themes that become key throughout the book or the ministry to which the person is called. In Jeremiah's case, God tells Jeremiah, 'I have set you this day over nations and over kingdoms, to pluck up and to break down, to destroy and to overthrow, to build and to plant' (Jer 1.10). This idea of plucking up, breaking down, destroying, overthrowing, building and planting becomes a theme throughout the book of Jeremiah and, indeed, Jeremiah's prophecies. Key motifs like this one give continuity to the text, but the main aim seems to be to highlight an important idea. In this case, when one reads about plucking up and breaking down, that is, the destruction of Judah, one also remembers 'building and planting' and thus that Judah's destruction is always in the context of restoration.

A key motif can also act as a rhetorical device. For instance, the 'foe from the north' mentioned in chapter 1 turns out to be Babylon, the powerful empire who subjugated nations to herself (1.14). When Babylon herself is thus threatened at the end of the book with a 'foe from the north' who will destroy her, the term brings irony to the text, for, until now, Babylon has been the foe from the north (50.9).

If you are someone who annotates your Bible, then, when you have finished reading this study, you might find it an informative and fun exercise to go through the Book of Jeremiah, chapter by chapter, highlighting with coloured pencils the various themes or phrases that are 'very Jeremiah.' It will help you keep your concentration on what you are reading and hopefully will give you a visual overview to these themes. For instance, you might want to highlight in blue 'foe from the north' and in orange references to plucking up, breaking down, building or planting. You might like to distinguish between the negative and positive actions here, however, so plucking up and breaking down might be in orange while building and planting are in green.

While the prophetic books have their own characteristics, most of the prophets preached a message of repentance. That is, they warned of God's judgment unless the people repented of their corruption. This was Jeremiah's message, which he faithfully preached for over forty years, but with his own distinct voice. One of the most remarkable aspects of Jeremiah's message is his consistent position that Judah needed to submit to Babylon. It was a message that seemed subversive, even treasonous, to his hearers and was a major reason that Jeremiah suffered so much for his message. The superscription at the beginning of the chapter has already given us the clue whether the people listened to Jeremiah, for Jeremiah preached 'until the exile of Jerusalem,' that is, until the nation of Judah was plucked up, broken down, destroyed and overthrown. Plucking up and breaking down is almost never God's last word in the Old Testament, however, and the building and planting was the reality beyond exile.

Jeremiah's Words

3

Plucking Up and Tearing Down: Sins and Sermons

We have looked at a couple of key themes in Jeremiah. One that is difficult to see for yourself without knowing Hebrew is the occurrence of the Hebrew word *shuv*, which can be translated as 'return,' 'repent,' or 'turn.' In addition, there are various forms of the word in Hebrew. It is a common word in the Old Testament, but Jeremiah uses it more than most and it is especially prominent in Jeremiah 3 (and 4), where restoration is offered to Israel (and Judah), conditional upon her returning (*shuv*) to the LORD. The corollary, of destruction if the people do not return/repent, is tempered with, 'Though I will not destroy it completely' (4.27 NIV).

The Temple Sermon (Jer 7.1-15)

Jeremiah 7.1–8.3, the first large chunk of prose in Jeremiah, is famously called, 'The Temple Sermon' because Jeremiah is called to preach in the gate of the LORD's house, the temple. This sermon (also summarized in the first part of chapter 26), introduces a favourite phrase in Jeremiah that is rarely used elsewhere: 'the LORD of Hosts, the God of Israel' (7.3). Whether intended or not, the double appellation reminds the reader that while God has elected Israel to be his particular people and has a covenant with them that he does not have with other nations, he is also LORD over everything in the universe—the hosts of galaxies, stars, planets and everything in between. Or, to put it the other way around, it reminds Israel that the one who is sovereign over everything is the one who has chosen Israel for his people.

The Temple Sermon focuses on some of the common themes in Jeremiah, such as: deception and falsehood (7.4, 8, 9); idolatry (7.6, 9; see also 18, 30–31; 8.2); justice, chiefly in terms of not oppressing the poor and weak, or shedding innocent blood (7.5-6); empty sacrifices, that is performing religious rituals while disobeying God (7.9–11; see also 21–23); and promises of wellbeing if the people repent (7.7). One could do worse than consider the Temple Sermon to be 'Jeremiah in a nutshell.'

The Temple Sermon takes issue with people who were unfaithful in their relationship to God, having offered sacrifices to false gods, and who were corrupt in their behaviour to others, yet still dared to think that they could enter into his temple. 'Will you steal, murder, commit adultery, swear falsely, make offerings to Baal, and go after other gods that you have not known, and then come and stand before me in this house, which is called by my name, and say, "We are delivered!"...?' (Jer 7.9–10). Some themes, such as justice and righteousness, are common to the other prophets and even the Old Testament in general. Right living as God's people was never to be a solely religious matter, such as making sacrifices to God, but involved honesty in business deals and standing up for the rights of the oppressed and marginalized. Temple worship became void if social justice was not upheld.

The people of Judah may have recited, 'The temple of the LORD' as a kind of talisman and taken comfort in the claim that they had on the temple (7.4). Given their lifestyles, however, these words are 'deceptive words' (that word, *sheqer*, again—v 4). Verse 8 repeats this same message even more starkly: 'Behold, you trust in deceptive words to no avail.' The people thought that with a bit of temple attendance they could quite literally get away with murder (verses 9–11). The hypocrisy that effectively makes mockery of the temple system triggers some of Jeremiah's strongest invectives. Similarly, this sort of false life is what upset Jesus about some of the Pharisees in the gospels. Jeremiah and Jesus were not against temple worship (or Pharisees). They were against empty or false temple worship.

Killer Kings and Phony Prophets (Jer 21–23, 27–28)

Jehoiakim's Injustice (Jer 22)

Many of the problems in the Book of Jeremiah were worse at the top of the social structure and the spotlight turns on King Jehoiakim (who reigned from 609 to 598 BCE) in chapter 22. Jehoiakim's father, Josiah, had led the reforms in Judah and while he was alive the nation followed him, but with his early death came a return to apostasy. Unlike Josiah, his successor and son Jehoiakim was a wicked man. His wickedness lay in his selfish lifestyle which led to a total disregard of human worth and life. This rich king wanted to build the most luxuriant palace he could and no expense was spared on the wood and the paint (22.14). Where he did cut costs was on labour; he did not pay his workers (22.13). In fact, it seems that his exploitation reached such levels that he shed innocent blood (22.17), unless the reference to shedding of innocent blood indicates another string to his bow of injustice, aside from his building project. Jehoiakim's desire was for his own wealth, acquired by any means, and to display it ostentatiously. The people he exploited and killed were his subjects that looked to him for protection from their enemies. Instead, their king was their enemy. In today's terms, we

Many of the problems in Jeremiah were worse at the top of the social structure

would say that Jehoiakim was financially and morally corrupt. Jehoiakim was the archetypal, hard-nosed, self-serving ruler who has no time whatsoever for those who presume to speak truth to power. Jehoiakim is contrasted with his father and 22.16 explicitly equates knowing God with pleading the cause of the afflicted and needy. This idea of knowing God being linked with, even equated to, living rightly is a theme that is found throughout Jeremiah (for example 4.22; 9.3, 5-6, 23–24; 31.31–34).

False Prophets (Jer 23, 27–28)

Judah's leaders are criticized more heavily than the common people, precisely because of the damage they do to the ordinary people. In Jehoiakim's case, that was physical exploitation. In the case of Jeremiah's fellow prophets, it is for leading people astray. They are accused of being false prophets, and chapters 23 and 27–28 are deeply concerned with such prophets and their message. The word for falsehood / deceit / lies (*sheqer*) occurs several times in these chapters.

The prophets of the northern kingdom (Samaria) prophesied 'by Baal' (23.13), that is 'They prophesied in the name of Baal' and led the people to follow this false God.[6] The sin of the southern kingdom (Jerusalem) prophets is that they walk in falsehood, supporting evildoers and discouraging repentance. In fact, instead of warning the people of judgment if they do not amend their ways, these false prophets reassure people that their future will be one of peace and that calamity will not come upon them (23.14–17).

Confusingly, some of these false prophets seem on first glance to be authentic. They claim to have had a visitation from God in their dreams, dreams being a valid way in the Old Testament by which God spoke to people. On further investigation, however, the words they speak belie their claims, for it is the word itself, not the mode of its transmission, that is of paramount importance: 'Let him who has my word speak my word faithfully' (23.28). In this case, the dreams are false and God's word is not being proclaimed. After all, anyone can say, 'God spoke to me in a dream.'[7]

> If you are highlighting in your Bible the various themes in Jeremiah, then take a look at the context in which 'false / falseness' and / or 'lying / lies' are used (both are used to translate *sheqer*). It is the prophets who come in for most criticism in this area.

Wrongs, Writes and Rewrites (Jer 36)

King Jehoiakim—he who had built his ostentatious red cedar palace by the blood of his people—comes into the story again in chapter 36, but he is no more inclined to the things of God than he was in chapter 22. As the scroll with God's words on it is read to him, he cuts it up and burns it. God simply tells Jeremiah to take another scroll and rewrite it and chapter 36 ends with Baruch rewriting at Jeremiah's dictation (see also 45.1).

There is irony in comparing the prophet Jeremiah with King Jehoiakim. Jeremiah, who describes God's words as a joy and a delight to his heart (Jer 15.16), elsewhere describes God's word to him as fire in his bones (Jer 20.9). These words burn him if he does not utter them. While Jeremiah is burnt by God's word, Jehoiakim burns God's word; the effect of God's word upon the prophet of faith and the unrighteous king is quite different. If God's words are fire, as Jeremiah perceives them to be, then Jehoiakim's attempt to burn them is as futile as trying to burn fire. Putting fire into fire simply makes a better fire and, indeed, the subsequent scroll had more words on it—bigger and better than the one that Jehoiakim had burnt.

Building and Planting (Jer 30–31)

Chapter 36 centres around the writing of a scroll dictated by Jeremiah and written by Baruch. The Book of Jeremiah says more about the writing and recording of God's word than other biblical books and two of Jeremiah's scribes, the brothers Baruch and Seraiah, are prominent figures. Jeremiah 30–31 is known as The Book of Consolation (or 'Comfort'); it is described as a 'book' because in 30.2 God tells Jeremiah to write his words in a book. Thus when we read in the Book of Consolation that God is going to write his law on the hearts of the people, it fits in with the theme throughout Jeremiah of writing down God's words (31.34). It also takes up the motif of the covenant in Jeremiah.

Jeremiah 30–31 is regarded as a book of consolation/ comfort because these chapters are full of hope

The reason that Jeremiah 30–31 is regarded as a book of consolation/comfort is because these chapters are full of hope. While Judah would not be able to escape the exile, she could look forward to a happier future and The Book of Consolation/Comfort envisages this restoration. 'As I have watched over them to pluck up and break down, to overthrow, destroy, and bring harm, so I will watch over them to build and to plant, declares the LORD' (Jer 31.28). Note the familiar theme of plucking up, breaking down, building and planting that we first encountered in Jeremiah's call (1.10).

In this Book of Comfort, we find the first reference in the Bible to the 'new covenant' (31.31). The covenant is important to Jeremiah and there are many references in the book to breaking it. The new covenant is a solution to the seeming inability of the people to keep the existing one. God will write it on their hearts so that it will be inherent to them. While Jeremiah is the only one in the Old Testament to talk explicitly about the new covenant, Ezekiel's new heart and new spirit (Ezek 36.26) has the same idea and there are passages in Isaiah with a similar theme, such as the 'new thing' God will do (Isa 43.19). While newness might imply new and different, it might be more helpful to think in terms of renewed, such as doing a screen refresh on a news' webpage to get the latest content.

Christians do, of course, rightly read the Old Testament in the light of the New Testament (and read the New Testament in the light of the Old Testament) and Christianity has usually seen the new covenant as linked with the death of Jesus. This is mainly from what Hebrews 8–9 says about the new covenant. It is important that Christians recognize and remember, however, both that Jeremiah 31 has its own context and that the Old Testament is Scripture to Jewish people who do not consider the New Testament and Jesus to be the fulfilment of what Jeremiah was talking about. Jeremiah's original context was the exile and the new covenant was a reiteration of the old one which the people broke, but in a way that the people would find easier to keep. For while the people might break the covenant, God could not break his covenant with David—the one covenant would endure (33.20–22). Those who adhere to Judaism would still understand Jeremiah's new covenant similarly today. When looked at through the lens of the cross and resurrection, however, as the writer of Hebrews does, the new covenant carries further meaning, including incorporating the gentiles, something that the writer of Jer 31.31 almost certainly did not envisage.[8]

4

Jeremiah's Life

Lament—Jeremiah's Mental Anguish (Jeremiah 20)

As we have already seen, Jeremiah's task was not easy. He was a single man, who had a tough, urgent message of judgment to deliver. God did not punish as Jeremiah kept saying he would, and it seems that Jeremiah was mocked for this (Jer 20.7, 10). He was a faithful messenger of God's word, but he was human. At various times in this first section of the Book of Jeremiah especially, Jeremiah expresses his discontent in what are known as Jeremiah's confessions or laments (11.18–12.6; 15.10–21; 17.14–18; 18.18–23 and 20.7–18).

Laments have an established form, or genre, in the OT and are found primarily in the Psalms, where they sit alongside songs of praise and other types of psalm.[9] Probably once used in liturgical settings, they have given voice to recurrent issues in the life of the faithful down through the ages.

In the lament of chapter 20, Jeremiah has been beaten and put in stocks for his preaching (Jer 20.2) and when he is released the next day, having uttered an unwelcome message against his accuser and tormenter, he laments his situation before God (Jer 20.7–13). He accuses God of deceiving him (20.7—although deception is a theme in Jeremiah, the word *sheqer* is not used in these few verses) and complains that his friends want him to be deceived (20.10). Yet he still remembers that the LORD is with him and will cause his persecutors to stumble. As psalms of lament often do, this passage ends on a positive note of trust in God for deliverance or praise for the help he is going to give. For Jeremiah 20.13 reads, 'Sing to the LORD; praise the LORD! For he has delivered the life of the needy from the hand of evildoers.' Except it does not end there.

Following this note of praise, Jeremiah plunges into a far more passionate outburst in which cursing is predominant (20.14–18). He curses the day that he was born and even curses the man who broke the good news of Jeremiah's birth to his father. Jeremiah wishes that he had never been born and had died in his mother's womb.[10] He is hurt, angry, despairing and thoroughly miserable. Although God does not reply, his response is to hear Jeremiah's misery and to keep hearing it down the years, the centuries, the millennia, for his words have been recorded forever.

Jeremiah's misery has been recorded forever

At this point it is worth clarifying what we can and cannot say about the kinds of psychological issues raised in passages such as these. Modern psychology and counselling stress the need to listen to people in pain and caution that replies are not always needed. Silence is sometimes the greater response—as, too, is memory in terms of remembering another's pain, and not assuming that they are soon over it. As one needs to be careful not to treat the Bible as a historical textbook, so one should beware of basing one's psychology entirely on the Bible. Not only was the biblical text not written to address issues in the recent field of psychology, but we live in a different time and culture. Nevertheless, lessons can be fruitfully learned by meditating on such texts.

The lament form is stylized, and if Jeremiah had a vocal outburst, it would have been highly unlikely to have been uttered in poetry. The poetic nature of the lament does not detract from its emotional nature, any more than love poetry diminishes the love felt by the writer. In fact, the reverse can be the case; poetry allows a fuller expression due to the type of language used in poetry, such as metaphors and exaggeration. Poetry, with other art forms, is sometimes reserved for the strongest emotions. Jeremiah's language is strong, but I would ask if Jeremiah is really asking God to destroy the man who brought news of his birth to his father (20.15–17). I would suggest not—but instead would propose that the words express the tone and thus the emotion that Jeremiah is experiencing.[11] It is the outburst of a man having a meltdown, to use colloquial language, and, as such, the words of Jer 20.15–17 are not to be taken as a serious request to heaven. If not Jeremiah's cursing, what about the other curses we find in the Old Testament, particularly the psalms? Might they, too, be outbursts of raw emotion, rather than reasoned requests and pleading petitions? It is worth considering seriously the possibility that one should read the imprecatory (cursing) psalms, such as Psalm 137, through the lens of Jer 20.15–17—that is, to read them as unchecked angry and hurt outbursts from those who take their situation and emotions to God in prayer, as opposed to acting rashly on their feelings.

Jeremiah's words are the outburst of a man having a meltdown

Symbolic Actions

Jeremiah did not simply preach and proclaim the message of God; he had to live the message. By that I mean more than that he simply had to live up to what he preached. This living out the message took two forms. First, he was to act out, symbolically, the lesson God wanted the people to hear in one-off actions. Jeremiah's buying of a worthless field because he trusted that in the future it would again be valuable is one such 'symbolic action' (32.6–25). It was to symbolize hope for the future (see 32.41–44). Wearing a linen loincloth that was then hidden in a rock crevice where it became ruined over time was to demonstrate the ruin of Judah's pride (Jer 13). Similarly, buying and breaking an earthenware jar was to emphasize to the people that God would break them (Jer 19). Other symbolic actions were: wearing straps and an oxen yoke around his neck (Jer 27–28); giving the Rechabites wine to drink (Jer 35); and hiding stones in the entrance to Pharaoh's palace (Jer 42).[12]

The second form of living out the message was in long-term life decisions. Notably, Jeremiah was not to marry or have children in order to demonstrate that God's judgment would bring an end to families (16.2). In a society where marriage was so much the norm that the OT has no word for bachelor, anyone seeing Jeremiah or thinking about him would probably be reminded of his message.[13] In addition, Jeremiah was not to mourn or to attend celebrations, at least for a time, which meant that he was prohibited from going to funerals and weddings (16.5, 8). This was also to show that celebrating, even mourning, would disappear. Other prophets had to demonstrate God's message through their marriages and family lives: see Isaiah 7, 8; Ezek 24.15–27; and Hosea 1–3.

While in many ways the impact of their vocation on the prophets' personal lives may seem strange, there are many believers today who, despite seeing it as a cost, remain single—and chaste—because they consider it is more glorifying to God. The 'cost of discipleship' (to use Bonhoeffer's well-known term) will be different from believer to believer, but to live completely for God is normally to encounter some cost, even though the same life usually brings joy, freedom and purpose.

God Engaged

5

Weeping Prophet or Weeping God

In some cases, such as Jeremiah 20, laments clearly belong to the prophet himself. In other instances, though, it is not clear if the tears are Jeremiah's or God's. Since the prophets spoke God's words on his behalf, the words of God and prophets are sometimes one and the same thing. Nevertheless, there are other times when the weeping belongs to God, even though the prophet is God's mouthpiece.

One such instance is in Jer 9.1: 'Oh that my head were waters, and my eyes a fountain of tears, that I might weep day and night for the slain of the daughter of my people!' As Patrick Miller notes of this passage, and it could be said of other similar passages:

> While it is customary to understand the speaker of these words as the prophet lamenting over the people, over "my people" (NRSV, "my poor people"), it is equally possible, as the context suggests, that we have here the voice of God.[14]

This is where it is important as readers to remember that scholars, even translators, are coming from their own specific cultural and gendered settings which might colour their interpretation. That is, a male, Western translator and interpreter might have found it unseemly to have a 'male' God crying.[15] Where the Hebrew naturally reads the tears as being God's, to give them to Jeremiah detracts from a fuller portrayal of who God is.

Later in the chapter, we read:

> I will take up weeping and wailing for the mountains, and a lamentation for the pastures of the wilderness, because they are laid waste so that no one passes through, and the lowing of cattle is not heard; both the birds of the air and the beasts have fled and are gone. I will make Jerusalem a heap of ruins, a lair of jackals, and I will make the cities of Judah a desolation, without inhabitant. (9.10–11).

God would judge and bring punishment on his people who refused to repent, but executing such punishment brings him pain. Terence Fretheim writes,

'For God, the internal side of judgment is grief.'[16] We shall see later that God weeps over Moab.

The Book of Jeremiah portrays a God who is deeply engaged with humans, particularly his people, Israel and Judah, but his weeping over them does not detract from God's power, holiness and sovereignty. To draw attention to his tears, however, is to insist on keeping a balance that has sometimes been lost.

A God Responsive to Humans

In a few places in Jeremiah (for example 7.16; 11.14) Jeremiah is told not to pray for the people. Many scholars (such as Brueggemann and McKeating) consider that this is because, to use Brueggemann's words, God is 'past listening.'[17] John Calvin, writing in the sixteenth century, suggested that it was in order that Jeremiah did not identify too closely with his nation, but instead carried out his role as a judge over them.[18] He also proposes that the people would have no ill will towards Jeremiah because it was not Jeremiah's decision, but God's.[19] Since the Fathers, however, another reason has sometimes been voiced. Ambrose, writing in the fourth century, declares that the LORD was moved by 'the intercession of the prophet and the entreaty of so great a seer.'[20] Patrick Miller, likewise, argues that intercessory prayer is so powerful that God will listen to it and will not do as he has threatened (see Exod 32.11–14 and Amos 7).[21] Indeed, if Jeremiah's pleas would be ineffective, why ban them?

In Jeremiah 18, Jeremiah goes down to the potter's house to watch him working and reworking his clay. This chapter explicitly makes clear the responsive relationship that God has with humans—primarily, and in the context of, his covenant with Israel. The passage describes how God can be influenced by people. If he has decided to punish a nation, but the people repent, then he will not punish them. Conversely, if he has decided to bless them, but they are wicked, then he will not bless them after all (18.7–10). Walter Moberly has written incisively on this chapter, arguing that while God makes it clear that he could treat the people as a potter treats clay and have no more interaction with them than a potter has with a piece of clay, he does not. Although he does have ultimate power, he curbs it and is responsive to human attitude and actions. Thus, 'This episode of the potter's house becomes a striking formulation of the relationship between divine sovereignty and human responsibility.'[22]

God can be influenced by people

6

The Others

As with the Old Testament in general, the Book of Jeremiah is concerned primarily with Judah / Israel. As is also characteristic of the Old Testament, there are times in Jeremiah when the outsider behaves better than the insider. The best example of this is the story of Ebed-Melech in Jeremiah 38.

Ebed-Melech

While we may think of Ebed-Melech as a name, the translation of this Hebrew epithet is 'servant of the king.' In other words, it might well be that the person remains unnamed throughout. What we do know of him is that he is an Ethiopian eunuch—a slave—who works in the king's palace. The text does not explicitly compare King Zedekiah with his slave, but it does paint two starkly different characters. King Zedekiah is, one might have thought, the most powerful man in the kingdom. Ebed-Melech is not only foreign, but a slave and even a eunuch—he does not have power. As the story unfolds, however, we see that Zedekiah runs afraid through the whole of the chapter. When the officials come to complain that they do not like Jeremiah's message and request his death, Zedekiah tells them that Jeremiah is in their hands, 'for the king can do nothing against you' (38.5). His weakness will see a man die. Ebed-Melech, on the other hand, on hearing that they had thrown Jeremiah into a cistern full of mud, seizes the opportunity that his position of servant of the king affords and dares to confront the king (38.7–8).

He does so immediately, going out of the palace to where the king is. He begins by addressing the king deferentially; 'My lord the king,' but then boldly accuses the officials of acting wickedly (38.9). He does not even make a request of the king, but simply says that Jeremiah's life is at risk in the cistern (38.9). Perhaps this is to maintain his position as a servant in submission. His actions could cost the slave his life and thus are brave and stand in contrast to the king's weak ones. Ebed-Melech's bravery saves the life of a man. Zedekiah's immediately positive response to Ebed-Melech, and his command (at least Zedekiah is still able to command his slaves!) to take thirty men to rescue one man from a cistern indicates that he either had not really wanted to go along with the officials in the first place, or has had a change of heart.

The pace of the narrative moves slowly through the rescue of Jeremiah from the cistern. Ebed-Melech, who clearly knows his way around the king's palace and has some authority, conducts the rescue mission (38.11). He first takes the men under his authority, then gathers the equipment he needs, delivers by ropes what Jeremiah needs down the well, and finally tells Jeremiah to put the rags and ropes under his armpits (38.12). Once Jeremiah has been pulled out of the cistern, Ebed-Melech drops out of the story. At the end of the next chapter, however, God gives a message through Jeremiah to this African servant to say that when he punishes Jerusalem, he will rescue Ebed-Melech and preserve his life, 'because you have put your trust in me' (39.18).

We might here be reminded of the prostitute Rahab who was saved at the fall of Jericho. The thread of the 'righteous gentile' runs throughout the OT and into the NT where the Parable of the Good Samaritan echoes that of Ebed-Melech. At the same time, the outsider behaving more righteously than the insider, or even rescuing the insider, may be a thread that runs through the canon, but it is not the main thrust of the OT, or the Bible as a whole.[23] Foreign nations behave in reprehensible ways and are included in God's judgment as the oracles against the nations make clear.

The Other Nations (Jer 46–51)

The oracles against the nations (OANs) are prophecies against, or concerning, the foreign nations, that is, non-Israelite and non-Judahite nations. Each of the major prophetic books—Isaiah, Jeremiah and Ezekiel—contain several chapters of OANs. In Jeremiah, the OANs comprise chapters 46–51 and deal in turn with: Egypt; Philistia; Moab; Ammon; Edom; Damascus (Aram); Kedar and the kingdoms of Hazor (Arabian tribes); Elam and Babylon. The Book of Jeremiah in the Greek translation of the Old Testament, the Septuagint, is one seventh shorter than the Hebrew Masoretic Text version and the OANs come in the middle of the book.[24] They follow on from chapter 25 which talks about the nations drinking the cup of the wine of the wrath of God.

Questions have been raised regarding why these OANs are in Israel's Scriptures. Probably, the nations concerned never heard the prophecies, so it seems that they might not have been intended for the nations to hear. Some have suggested that judgment against the nations meant salvation to Israel and it does appear that this is one important theme—Judah receives a salvation oracle at the end of Egypt's prophecy of judgment (Jeremiah 46). At the same time, in the climate where Babylon was the threat, Ammon's and Moab's demises had little positive impact on Judah. Others have suggested that the OANs show to his chosen people that God is sovereign over all the nations and has dealings with others. These oracles also demonstrate to God's people that it was not only they who were being punished. There may well be more than one reason that prophecies against other nations are included in the OT and even different reasons across the OANs.[25]

The OAN against Babylon takes up two of the six OAN chapters (Jeremiah 50–51 in the Hebrew). Babylon is the shadowy foe from the north, which first makes her appearance in Jeremiah in the first chapter. She is the nation that becomes God's cup of wrath in chapter 25 from which all other nations are to drink and she is the land of exile into which the Judahites are taken when Judah is conquered.

God refers twice to 'Nebuchadnezzar, the king of Babylon, my servant' (Jer 27.6; 43.10) and God uses Babylon to punish other nations, but in the end he punishes her, too. On first glance, therefore, it may appear that Babylon has an ambiguous relationship with God. A closer look at what is meant by 'my servant' helps give a better perspective of the situation. Babylon at the end of the seventh century and beginning of the sixth century BCE was the prevalent empire in the Ancient Near East and nations had to submit to her. It would have been easy for people to think that there was no one greater or stronger than Babylon. 'My servant' demonstrates that the LORD was the one who was ultimately in control and that Babylon did nothing that God did not allow. God was sovereign, not King Nebuchadnezzar. That powerful king was but a servant, whether or not he recognized it. Later God describes Babylon as his war-club with which he destroys nations (51.20). It should have been comforting for Judah to know that she was in the hands of a just God who had limits and not in the hands of a cruel empire who might never have compassion.

One reason that Babylon draws God's attention is because of her treatment of his people, for an offence against God's people was offence against God himself. 'All who found them have devoured them, and their enemies have said, "We are not guilty, for they have sinned against the LORD, their habitation of righteousness, the LORD, the hope of their fathers"' (50.7). Babylon may have thought that she was being used to punish God's people and was therefore not guilty, but that was not God's view. God might have used Babylon for his own purposes in judging the surrounding nations, but at no point did that make Babylon innocent, which may be why the longest OAN is reserved for her, 'For she has sinned against the LORD' (50.14). She will be repaid according to all she has done (50.29).

God used Babylon for his own purposes in judging the nations

With Babylon's demise comes the release for the other nations she has oppressed. With the irony that is typical of Old Testament narrative, the foe from the north will be destroyed by her own foe from the north (51.48). At the end of chapter 51, the scroll with the prophecy of Jeremiah 50–51 is sunk with a stone in the middle of the Euphrates. The action is to act as an object lesson: Babylon herself will sink, never to rise again.

Apart from the oracle concerning Babylon in chapters 50–51, the oracle against Moab in chapter 48 is the longest of the foreign nation oracles in Jeremiah. This oracle is of especial interest because in this oracle, God cries over Moab (see particularly 48.31–39), a foreign nation and, moreover, one that does not repent. Moab is the only foreign nation over which God weeps. In OT prophecy there is often what is termed 'the language of the law courts.' People are accused of various sins, then comes a 'therefore' after which comes God's sentence—the punishment which he will mete out. In Jer 48.29, we learn of some of Moab's sins of which she is accused—her extreme pride (words for pride or arrogance are used six times in the verse)—and verse 30 continues in the same vein.

Then in verse 31, comes that fateful pivot, 'Therefore.' Where one would expect God's judgment to fall, however, God's tears fall instead, 'Therefore, I wail for Moab; I cry out for all Moab; for the men of Kir-hareseth I mourn. More than for Jazer I weep for you, O vine of Sibmah!' (Jer 48.31–32). The following verses in Jeremiah 48 go on to outline the judgment that will fall on Moab and I would suggest that God weeps because of the punishment that he is about to inflict. 'I will bring to an end in Moab, declares the LORD, him who offers sacrifice in the high place and makes offerings to his god. Therefore my heart moans for Moab' (48.35–36). Jeremiah's oracle against Moab demonstrates that grief is the internal side of judgment for those who are not God's chosen people—and even those who are enemies of God. Moab made herself an enemy of God because she made his people a derision (48.27) and, as with Babylon, that alone was enough to turn God's eye of judgment in her direction.

If I were to preach Jeremiah 48 then I might make a link at this point to Rom 5.8: 'God shows his love for us in that while we were still sinners, Christ died for us.' This would be an example of how I look at an OT text through the lens of the cross and the resurrection.

The End, the Conclusion and Beyond

7

The End of the Book of Jeremiah (Jer 52)

Once the scroll has been dropped into the Euphrates and Seraiah (at Jeremiah's command) has declared that Babylon will sink never to rise again, the chapter ends with, 'Thus far are the words of Jeremiah' (51.64). This implies that the Book of Jeremiah is at an end. It is not the first time that one might have expected the Book of Jeremiah to end, for chapter 45, where Baruch is given his life as a reward, would have nicely finished the book. As the OANs followed after chapter 45, however, so there is a further chapter here, and one which acts as an addendum to the book. Jeremiah 52 is very similar to 2 Kings 25 and is an account of Jerusalem's fall to Babylon. Babylon's own fall lies in the future, yet the Book of Jeremiah ends with a glimmer of hope for Judah. The Judahite king Jehoiachin (son of Jehoiakim) who has previously been taken into exile, finds favour with the Babylonian king and eats at his table for the rest of his life. God still has his hand on the broken people, and King Jehoiachin's status in the land of exile is the first seedling in the next phase of planting and building.

Conclusion

The Book of Jeremiah could be summed up in various ways, but perhaps one way of summarizing his message would be, 'walk the talk'—the people were to live a life in keeping with their faith. For the Judahites that meant worshipping only one God and treating one's fellow human beings justly and rightly, especially the poor, oppressed and afflicted. The Judahites had a king who oppressed his people to the point of bloodshed and their prophets taught lies. The corruption was endemic and thorough and so God sent them into exile in Babylon. He did the same with the other nations and even Babylon, herself, was soon cast down. The promise of building up as outlined in the Book of Comfort was a hope that could sustain the people while in exile.

Jeremiah was a faithful and true prophet, but he suffered for it. If he feels remote to us with his buying and breaking pots, and not attending weddings, then his anguish in chapter 20 brings him into our realm as a man with a breaking point. Jeremiah did not reach that breaking point. His outburst in chapter 20 may have helped him keep going. He reminds us, however, that there are suffering servants of God and they need our prayers.

My own prayer for you is that you come to have a deepening appreciation of the Book of Jeremiah, the other prophetic books, the Old Testament in general and, finally, the Bible as a whole. My prayer is also that, ultimately, your study of Scripture will lead to a deeper love and respect for the LORD of hosts, the God of Israel—the God that the prophet Jeremiah spent his life serving so faithfully.

Further Reading

Jeremiah Commentaries

D P Miller, 'Jeremiah,' in *Isaiah—Ezekiel, The New Interpreter's Bible: A Commentary in Twelve Volumes*, vol 6 (Nashville, TN: Abingdon Press, 2001)—my first choice of commentary in a good commentary series. The biblical text is written out and then there is a commentary section followed by a reflection. It is just the right length and pitch for a beginning student of Jeremiah, as well as being a good resource for those who know more.

T E Fretheim, *Jeremiah*, Smyth and Helwys Bible Commentary series (Macon, GA: Smyth and Helwys, 2002)

R E Clements, *Jeremiah*, 'Interpretation' series (Atlanta, GA: John Knox, 1988)

W A Brueggemann, *A Commentary on Jeremiah: Exile and Homecoming* (Cambridge: William B Eerdmans, 1998).

D O Wenthe (ed), *Ancient Christian Commentary on Scripture: Jeremiah and Lamentations*, Vol XII (Downers Grove, IL: IVP, 2009)—worth reading on more than one level. As it says on the cover, it is full of snippets from ancient Christian commentators. So, for instance, Theodoret of Cyr writing on Jehoiakim's burning of the scroll in Jeremiah 36 says, 'The sheet of paper was burned, but the divine law remained unharmed. So also when the body assumed by the Word suffered, the Word remained free from suffering.'[26]

Interpretation

R Alter, *The Art of Biblical Narrative* (US: Basic Books, 1981)—a highly engaging classic on the fascinating subject of how texts are written and the significances of departures from the patterns.

E Davis, 'Teaching the Bible Confessionally in the Church,' in E F Davis and R B Hays (eds), *The Art of Reading Scripture* (Grand Rapids, MI: Eerdmans, 2003). This volume has a number of very good essays on reading the Bible as a Christian with academic integrity. Ellen Davis is always a good read.

R W L Moberly, *Prophecy and Discernment* (Cambridge University Press, 2006)—a contribution to his lifelong engagement with reading Scripture well.

T E Fretheim, *The Suffering of God: An Old Testament Perspective*, Overtures to Biblical Theology (Philadelphia, PA: Fortress Press, 1984)—valuable to be read in conjunction with the prophetic books. Fretheim is not afraid to keep the tears in God's eyes, rather than putting them in the prophet's; a perspective that has sometimes been lost.

Notes

1 A brief explanation of deuteronomistic history and editors is given in J J Collins, *Introduction to the Hebrew Bible* (Minneapolis, MN: Fortress Press, 2018, third edition) pp 187–188.

2 For example, Jer 23.5–6 is depicted as poetry in the NIV and the NASB, but as prose in the ESV and the NRSV.

3 An accessible introduction is given in J J Collins, *Introduction to the Hebrew Bible, op cit,* pp 504–505.

4 E Davis, 'Teaching the Bible Confessionally in the Church,' in E F Davis and R B Hays (eds), *The Art of Reading Scripture* (Grand Rapids, MI: Eerdmans, 2003) p 15.

5 N Habel analyzes call narratives, including Jeremiah's, and sets out their literary pattern in his paper, 'The Form and Significance of the Call Narratives,' Zeitschrift für die alttestamentliche Wissenschaft 77 (1965) pp 297–323.

6 W C Kaiser, with T Rata Jr, *Walking the Ancient Paths: A Commentary on Jeremiah* (Bellingham, WA: Lexham Press, 2019) p 283.

7 A further discussion of false prophecy in Jer 23.9–22 can be found in R W L Moberly, 'Jeremiah: the formulation of criteria for discernment,' in *Prophecy and Discernment* (Cambridge University Press, 2000) pp 70–82. In fact, as the title suggests, the whole book is pertinent to the discussion.

8 A good discussion of the new/old covenant can be found in S L McKenzie, *Covenant*, Understanding Biblical Themes (St Louis, MO: Chalice Press, 2000).

9 For an introduction to psalm forms, or types, see J J Collins, *Introduction to the Hebrew Bible, op cit,* pp 497–503.

10 Job, in the midst of his extreme suffering, laments similarly in Job 3.

11 Some recent scholarship, notably D A Lambert, *How Repentance Became Biblical: Judaism, Christianity, and the Interpretation of Scripture* (Oxford University Press, 2016), has challenged the extent to which OT language handles emotion in the way we do today. While the caution is helpful, I do not think this means we cannot talk about emotion in the text.

12 Kaiser, *Walking the Ancient Paths, op cit,* gives a brief but good introduction to Jeremiah's symbolic actions (pp 183–184). For further elucidation, I suggest taking each symbolic action in turn as given by Kaiser and Rata and looking it up in P D Miller's 'Jeremiah,' in *Isaiah—Ezekiel, The New Interpreter's Bible: A Commentary in Twelve Volumes*, vol 6 (Nashville, TN: Abingdon Press, 2001).

13 P C Craigie, in P C Craigie, P H Kelley and J F Drinkard, *Jeremiah 1–25*, Word Biblical Commentary, vol 26 (Dallas, TX: Word Books, 1991) p 216.

14 Miller, 'Jeremiah,' *op cit,* p 648.

15 I put 'male' in inverted commas to denote that while male pronouns are used of God, it does not necessarily follow that God is male.

16 T E Fretheim, *The Suffering of God: An Old Testament Perspective*, Overtures to Biblical Theology (Philadelphia, PA: Fortress Press, 1984) p 112; T E Fretheim, *Jeremiah*, Smyth and Helwys Bible Commentary (Macon, GA: Smyth and Helwys, 2002) pp 597, 602, 603.

17 W Brueggemann, *A Commentary on Jeremiah: Exile and Homecoming* (Grand Rapids, MI: Eerdmans, 1998) p 81; H McKeating, *The Book of Jeremiah*, Epworth Commentaries (Peterborough: Epworth Press, 1999) p 58.

18 J Calvin, *Jeremiah 1-19*, Calvin's Commentaries, vol 9 (Grand Rapids, MI: Baker Books, 2005, reprinted from the Calvin Translation Society) pp 383.

19 *ibid*, pp 383-384.

20 Ambrose quoted in D O Wenthe (ed), *Jeremiah, Lamentations*, Ancient Christian Commentary on Scripture, vol 12 (Downers Grove, IL: IVP, 2009) p 67.

21 Miller, 'Jeremiah,' *op cit*, p 638 (quotation), also p 670.

22 Moberly, *Prophecy and Discernment, op cit,* pp 48-55, quotation p 51.

23 For a fuller discussion of this topic, see F A Spina, *Faith of the Outsider: Exclusion and Inclusion in the Biblical Story* (Grand Rapids, MI: Eerdmans, 2005).

24 Protestant English Bibles are based on the Hebrew version.

25 For a fuller discussion, see my work: J Woods, *Jeremiah 48 as Christian Scripture* (Eugene, OR: Pickwick, 2011) pp 132-139; 173-180.

26 Wenthe, *Jeremiah, Lamentations, op cit,* p 233.